TABLE OF CONTENTS

THIS PAGE INTENTIONALLY LEFT BLANK

LIST OF FIGURES

iii

THIS PAGE INTENTIONALLY LEFT BLANK

LIST OF TABLES

THIS PAGE INTENTIONALLY LEFT BLANK

LIST OF ACRONYMS AND ABBREVIATIONS

ACI	Andean Counterdrug Initiative
ADAM	Areas for Municipal-Level Alternative Development
AUC	United Self-Defense Forces of Colombia
CRS	Congressional Research Service
DEA	Drug Enforcement Agency
DIRAN	Directorate of Antinarcotics
DNE	National Directorate of Narcotics
DoD	Department of Defense
DoS	State Department
ELN	National Liberation Army
FARC	Revolutionary Armed Forces of Colombia
FFWP	Family Forest Warden Program
FMF	Foreign Military Financing
GAO	Government Accountability Office
GME	Mobile Eradication Group
GNP	Gross National Product
GOC	Government of Colombia
IMET	International Military Education and Training
INL	Bureau of International Narcotics and Law Enforcement
MIDAS	Additional Investment for Sustainable Alternative Development
NADR	Nonproliferation, Antiterrorism, and Demining Related
NAS	Narcotics Affairs Section
NGO	Nongovernmental Organization
UN	United Nations
UNODC	United Nations Office on Drugs and Crime
USAID	United States Agency for International Development
USD	United States Dollars
WWII	World War II

THIS PAGE INTENTIONALLY LEFT BLANK

ACKNOWLEDGMENTS

I would like to express sincere gratitude to the United States Army Medical Department, which provided this educational opportunity to expand my professional and personal growth. In particular, I would like to thank COL Bruce McVeigh and COL Thomas Murphy, for their endorsement for my selection to attend the Naval Postgraduate School. I would also like to thank the many professors at the Naval Postgraduate School whose insight and knowledge guided me through their outstanding master's degree program.

I owe the largest debt to my lovely wife, Rosemarie, and our four children, Christian, Sebastian, Jonah, and Noah, for their continued sacrifice during my career endeavors. I would also like to thank my parents, Charles and Kathleen Catalano, for instilling in me the values of hard work and perseverance.

THIS PAGE INTENTIONALLY LEFT BLANK

I. INTRODUCTION

A. MAJOR RESEARCH QUESTION

The United States pursues several methods of promoting national security. The most publicized method involves direct U.S. intervention, as pursued in Afghanistan and Iraq. Today, the government is returning to a more indirect approach following a decade of direct involvement in two wars in which the U.S. experienced mixed results. A second method of promoting national security that is frequently utilized is the hardening of U.S. targets. Stricter travel laws, border control, personnel searches, and increased security are all aspects of this method. While shown to be an effective method of reducing security threats, this method does nothing to disrupt security threats at the source or "venue" states abroad.[1] The third and most broadly employed method of combating transnational threats uses the United States' influence and foreign assistance to enhance other nations' efforts. Foreign assistance and its effects on transnational threats within a recipient nation is the least understood of the three methods as it has traditionally been difficult to measure the success of the many programs the U.S. has undertaken. The history of U.S. foreign policy is dotted with successes and failures in the application of foreign assistance when pursuing national security objectives.

Following the devastation of World War II (WWII), European economies were in a state of complete disrepair. Understanding the importance of a healthy European economy, both to deter the spread of communism and alleviate widespread poverty, the United States embarked on a grand design to accelerate the European economy's recovery. The proposal to Congress was named the Marshall Plan, after then Secretary of State George C. Marshall.[2] The plan, as an extension of the communism containment strategy of the Truman Doctrine, would provide food, fuel, machinery, and other staples to rebuild transportation, agricultural, and industrial capabilities in Europe. President Harry Truman believed that such provisions would support "economic stability and

---

[1] Konstantinos Drakos and Andreas Gofas, "In Search of the Average Transnational Terrorist Attack Venue," *Defence and Peace Economics* 17, 2 (2006): 73.

[2] As presented to Congress, the Marshall Plan was originally titled the European Recovery Program

orderly political processes opposing the spread of chaos and extremism, preventing advancement of Communist influence and use of armed minorities, and orienting other foreign nations toward the U.S. and the U.N."[3] Scholars generally agree that the Marshall Plan succeeded by "eradicating the social and political and economic conditions on which Communism thrives."[4] The Marshall Plan administered approximately $13 billion in aid between 1949 and 1951 to sixteen European nations. It succeeded in bolstering Western Europe's economy as it realized a 40% industrial production increase beyond pre-war levels.[5] Additionally, communist influence in France and Italy were reduced while communist incursions in Greece and Turkey were deterred as security aid was successfully prioritized for those nations.[6] As the Marshall Plan concluded it morphed into the Mutual Security Act, which continued similar communism containment objectives through economic assistance. The Mutual Security Act eventually transitioned to the United States Agency for International Development (USAID) under the Kennedy Administration.

While the Marshall Plan is widely viewed as a foreign assistance success story within the realm of anticommunism foreign policy, a similar effort was made in South America with significantly poorer results. In 1961, President John F. Kennedy initiated the Alliance for Progress. Its charter enumerated 94 goals that would "achieve a real economic growth rate of at least 2.5 percent per capita (GNP) per year for participating Latin American nations.[7] Ancillary objectives involving improvements in education, employment, health, trade diversification, and government reform were to be completed by 1970. Similar to the Marshall Plan, Kennedy's aim was to diminish the economic and social conditions that would allow communism to take hold in Latin America. He

---

[3] William C. Cromwell, "The Marshall Non-Plan, Congress and the Soviet Union," *Western Political Quarterly*32, no. 4 (1979): 425.

[4] Greg Behrman, *The Most Noble Adventure: The Marshall Plan and the Time When America Helped Save Europe* (New York: Free Press, 2007), 328.

[5] A.E. Jeffcoat, "Dollars for Europe," *Wall Street Journal,* April 11, 1951, 1.

[6] Greece and Turkey received more than $500 million in security aid and military equipment between 1949 and 1951.

[7] Stephen C. Rabe, *The Most Dangerous Area in the World—John F. Kennedy Confronts Communist Revolution in Latin America* (Chapel Hill: The University of North Carolina Press, 1999), 148.

strongly believed that "the transformation of Latin America would justify U.S. global leadership and demonstrate the nation's ability to accomplish enlightened, anti-Communist policies."[8] The Alliance for Progress administered $22.3 billion between 1961 and 1973 to 19 South American countries.[9] Between 1961 and 1967 recipient nations experienced no significant gains in per capita economic growth. 1968 marked the first year per capita growth exceeded 2.5%.[10] Unemployment increased from 18 million in 1961 to 25 million in 1970. While agricultural output increased, it failed to adequately address the growing population. Similarly, health, education, income inequality reduction, and standard of living goals were not met.[11] Additionally, government reform goals were thwarted by "six military coups that overthrew elected governments in Argentina, Peru, Guatemala, Ecuador, the Dominican Republic, and Honduras."[12] The U.S. government's willingness to continue assistance to dictatorial governments led many South American nations to openly doubt the validity of Alliance for Progress's commitment to social reform and democracy. Although it was intended to counter the Cuban Revolution, scholars generally agree that the Alliance for Progress contributed to a less stable Latin America by failing to meet its lofty expectation and tacitly supporting military coups that ousted elected governments.[13] Foreign assistance continued to be used primarily as a communism containment strategy, with resources provided to Latin American and African nations for that purpose, until the early 1990s when the Soviet Union collapsed.

The United States has used foreign assistance to advance similar international security objectives in the last decade. Recent programs rely more heavily on security assistance, although economic assistance is still a large component. Both the 2006 and

---

[8] Ibid.

[9] Peter H. Smith, *Talons of the Eagle: Dynamics of U.S.-Latin American Relations* (New York: Oxford University Press, 1996), 152.

[10] Jerome Levinson and Juan de Onis, *The Alliance That Lost Its Way* (Chicago: Quadrangle Books, 1970), 8.

[11] Ibid., 10.

[12] Thomas C. Wright, *Latin America in the Era of the Cuban Revolution* (Westport: Praeger Publishers, 2001), 69.

[13] Ibid., 68–69.

2010 National Security Strategies label failed states and weak states as global hazards in a deeply interconnected world. In such states, governments are unable or unwilling to deter the activities of transnational actors. The Clinton, G. W. Bush , and Obama administrations have attempted to use economic and security assistance to encourage recipient governments to actively combat drug trafficking and other transnational threats. Foreign assistance that improves weak states' economic and security shortfalls is believed to be mutually beneficial to the recipient nation and the United States. Military partnerships and economic and security assistance are combined to form a comprehensive security strategy that "requires both more effort to build appropriate civilian capacity and better preparation of military forces to fill gaps that will inevitably appear by conducting or participating in political, social, information, and economic programs."[14]

In the last twenty years, terrorism and narco-trafficking are the two transnational threats that have received the most foreign assistance funding. While the results from counterterror initiatives are not yet clear, counter narcotics programs have yielded a wealth of data to allow for the analysis of specific foreign assistance programs.

Frequently referred to as non-lethal targeting by the military, the employment of USAID and the use of military forces and government agencies to enhance civil capacity when directed toward major drug producing nations and regions has been included as a significant aspect of the U.S. National Security Strategy over the last two decades.[15] The 2012 National Drug Control Strategy identifies transnational criminal organizations that import illicit drugs to the U.S. as a "persistent and dangerous threat to public health and safety."[16] It further states that international drug control measures are required to curb the amount of illicit narcotics brought into the U.S. Pursuing cooperative counter narcotic initiatives in countries such as Mexico and Colombia are envisioned as a way

---

[14] Richard A. Lacquement Jr., "Integrating Civilian and Military Activities." *Parameters* 40, no. 1 (2010): 10.

[15] White House, National Security Strategy of the United States (Washington, DC: White House, 1993), 18-19; White House, A National Security Strategy for a New Century (Washington, DC: White House, 1997), 4; White House, The National Security Strategy of the United States of America (Washington, DC: White House, 2002), 10; White House, The National Security Strategy of the United States of America (Washington, DC: White House, 2006), 48; White House, National Security Strategy (Washington, DC: White House, 2010), 42–43.

[16] White House, National Drug Control Strategy (Washington, DC: White House, 2012), 25.

toward "reducing the supply of illicit drugs in the United States while assisting nations that are adversely affected by the illicit drug trade."[17] The planned method of execution involves security agreements with international partners that are plagued with significant illicit crop cultivation and drug production. President Obama's plan incorporates security, economic, and governmental reforms within venue states that are "ultimately designed to reduce drug production and trafficking, promote alternative livelihoods, and strengthen rule of law, democratic institutions, citizen security, and respect for human rights."[18]

Though not as grand in scale as the Marshall Plan, several large interagency projects have been undertaken by the U.S. government in the last decade. Mostly skewed toward security assistance, modern projects include a mix of both security and economic assistance. Plan Colombia was initiated by the Clinton administration to assist the Colombian government with counter-narcotics, governing capacity, and economic development with the expressed intent of reducing drug trafficking into the U.S.[19] An assessment of the effectiveness of this program can provide insight into the strategic efficaciousness of foreign aid as a national security tool. How, if at all, has this initiative contributed to national security and a reduction in narcotic trafficking?

B. IMPORTANCE

National security has been strongly linked to foreign aid since the onset of the Cold War. Economic and security assistance were historically administered with anti-communism objectives in mind. In the 1980s and '90s the war on drugs supplanted the dwindling communist threat. The focus of foreign assistance shifted again after September 11, 2001, when counter-terrorism became the chief security concern. Through all the shifting priorities the strategy for applying assistance has remained largely the same without any real analysis of whether the old strategy fits the new threat environment. In the fiscally strained economy of the U.S. today, annual foreign

---

[17] Ibid., 31.

[18] Ibid.

[19] "United States Support for Colombia," March 28, 2000,
http://www.state.gov/www/regions/wha/colombia/fs_000328_plancolombia.html

5

assistance outlays of more than $35 billion (of which $10.3 billion is devoted specifically for peace and security) receives significant scrutiny and its effectiveness is often questioned. It is important that policy makers understand the impacts of foreign assistance pursuant to national security goals in order to determine whether such programs should receive further funding and if similar programs should be enacted elsewhere. Additionally, it is important to understand the settings in which the economic and developmental components of foreign assistance are more likely to yield the desired results than the security focused components. This thesis contributes to advancing such understanding.

C.   PROBLEMS AND HYPOTHESES

The argument presented in this thesis is that economic assistance is more effective at reducing drug trafficking than security assistance. This argument similarly stems from motivations. Drug crop cultivators are seeking financial security. Scholarly studies indicate that providing equitable alternatives sources of income to illicit crop farmers will reduce the amount of coca being cultivated.[20]

D.   LITERATURE REVIEW

Evaluating the success of foreign assistance programs has been a challenge for U.S. policy makers since the initiation of the Marshall Plan. The government and scholars alike have found it difficult to identify a causal relationship between aid and security objectives. There is a debate in the literature on the impact of foreign assistance as a tool for national security to date. One school of thought argues for significant positive effects, while another argues that impacts have been largely irrelevant and oftentimes negative. Several books and scholarly journal articles assert that U.S. economic and military aid programs help legitimize a weak state, further enabling the

---

[20] Gary S. Becker, "Crime and Punishment: An Economic Approach," *Journal of Political Economy* 76, no. 2 (March 1968): 169–217.

government to project power to the rural areas of their country. Authors of these works similarly claim that sustainable developmental assistance can promote U.S. strategic interests abroad.[21]

The basis of their argument lies in economic reasoning. When foreign governments fail or cannot provide basic services (rule of law, education, health care, etc.) their citizens are "likely to experience steeply escalating problems that spill over to the rest of the world, including the United States."[22] If the assistance is used effectively and prevents the disintegration of state institutions and governance, it will lead to greater power projection within a nation's borders. Greater power projection will allow the governments to prevent criminal organizations from using their country as a narcotics production factory. Additionally, economic benefits seek to dissuade would-be illicit crop farmers. Young men (a primary recruiting pool of criminal organizations and guerilla groups) are less likely to become disillusioned and engage in criminal activity if economic prospects exist within their community. Ultimately, a country that improves upon its civil liberty, economic, and security shortfalls is less likely to fall prey to violence from its own people, as well.[23] Unfortunately, while there are several articles extolling the importance of foreign assistance, few articles attempt to evaluate its impact using empirical evidence.[24] Of the few articles that do utilize empirical evidence, there is polarization among opinions regarding the effectiveness of foreign assistance as a tool to pursue strategic security objectives.

The use of aid to assist recipient nations with the eradication of drug crops has been a constant foreign policy practice since the Nixon administration. Very few

---

[21] Daniel Byman, *The Five Front War* (Hoboken: John Wiley & Sons, 2008), 194–195; Tom H. Hastings, *Nonviolent Response to Terrorism* (Jefferson: McFarland & Company, 2004), 4; Patrick M. Cronin, "Foreign Aid," in *Attacking Terrorism: Elements of a Grand Strategy,* ed. Audrey Kurth Cronin et al. (Washington, D.C.: Georgetown University Press, 2004), 248–249.

[22] Jeffrey D. Sachs, "The Strategic Significance of Global Inequality," *Washington Quarterly* 24, no. 3 (2001): 187–198.

[23] Royal C. Gardner, *International Assistance, Sustainable Development, and the War on Terrorism* (Washington, D.C.: Environmental Law Institute, 2002) 8; Jean-Paul Azam and Veronique Thelen. "The Roles of Foreign Aid and Education in the War on Terror." *Public Choice* 135, no. 3-4 (2008): 375–397.

[24] Cynthia Lum, Leslie W. Kennedy, and Alison Sherley. "Are Counter-Terrorism Strategies Effective? the Results of the Campbell Systematic Review on Counter-Terrorism Evaluation Research." *Journal of Experimental Criminology* 2, no. 4 (2006): 508–512.

empirical studies address the effectiveness of foreign aid in reducing drug trafficking. Due to the covert nature of narcotics transactions, scholars are limited to estimations based on coca, poppy, and cannabis cultivation quantities.

The concept of utilizing foreign assistance to curb illicit crop cultivation is heavily influenced by a widely cited 1968 study by Gary S. Becker titled "Crime and Punishment—An Economic Approach." Becker's findings support the belief that a cost-benefit analysis heavily influences why many people choose to commit crimes.[25]

> A person commits an offense if the expected utility to him exceeds the utility he could get by using his time and other resources at other activities. Some persons become "criminals," therefore, not because their basic motivation differs from that of other persons, but because their benefits and costs differ.[26]

Providing a legitimate alternative means of employment can therefore reduce the probability that a person will choose to commit a crime.[27] For a South American farmer with no access to legitimate agricultural markets, the choice to plant illicit crops is an easy one. A strong demand for illicit crops, a severely limited government presence, and scarce opportunities to make equivalent legal revenue all contribute to a farmer's decision to choose the criminal route to making money. If a government can minimize these barriers to legitimate employment than the likelihood that farmers will choose the illegal route is significantly diminished.

In 1998, Graham Farrell published "A Global Empirical Review of Drug Crop Eradication and United Nations Crop Substitution and Alternative Development Strategies." His article analyzed the effectiveness of crop substitution and illicit crop eradication in 11 different countries from 1970 through 1990. Eradication refers to the manual uprooting or fumigation of unwanted crops. Alternative development/substitution involves the replacement of illicit crops with legitimate ones. Through a multiyear comparison of the net income per hectare of alternative crops versus

---

[25] According to the Encyclopedia Britannica, a cost-benefit analysis is determined by dividing the projected benefits of a program [decision] by the projected costs.

[26] Becker, "Crime and Punishment," 176.

[27] Ibid., 177.

illicit crops (coca, poppy, and cannabis) Farrell demonstrated that alternative substitution was a viable option when government funding assisted the farmers in establishing new crops. His findings point to higher levels of crop substitution success when the government assists with the significant costs associated with upgrading to a legitimate agricultural product. Typically, improved infrastructure (roads, irrigation), seeds, fertilizers, pesticides, and hired labor were provided to ease the transition. The less successful countries failed to assist their farmers with the switch to a legitimate source of income. Paul T. Cohen and Joseph L. Zentner conducted similar data analysis with analogous results.[28]

Using data from 2001 to 2005, Michelle Dion and Katherine Russler conducted a five-year study of fumigation efforts in Colombia. Contrary to Farrell's findings, they concluded that fumigation does not reduce the amount of illicit crops being cultivated. Instead it succeeds in displacing coca farmers and coca plots to more remote locations that are smaller and less prone to government interference.[29] Additionally, they found that the extensive fumigation efforts did little to impact the market price and subsequent demand for cocaine.

In a 2006 study, Stella M. Rouse and Moises Arce analyzed the effects of U.S. counter narcotic policy on coca cultivation in Peru, Bolivia, and Colombia. Using data from 1980 to 2001, they performed a pooled cross-sectional time-series analysis while controlling for exogenous variables. U.S. security assistance was the independent variable under investigation and coca cultivation (measured in hectares) was the dependent variable. The data indicated that coca cultivation decreased in Peru and Bolivia, but not in Colombia when security assistance was provided. They concluded that narco-terror groups such as Revolutionary Armed Forces of Colombia (FARC) were

---

[28] Paul T. Cohen, "The Post-Opium Scenario and Rubber in Northern Laos: Alternative Western and Chinese Models of Development," *International Journal of Drug Policy* 20, no. 5 (2009): 424–430; Joseph L. Zentner, "The 1972 Turkish Opium Ban: Needle in the Haystack Diplomacy? [Efforts to Curtail Production; Effects on the Illicit Drug Market; Effects on the Turkish Economy; Efforts to Aid Poppy Farmers Affected by the Ban]," *World Affa*irs 136, (1973): 36–47.

[29] Michelle, L. Dion and Catherine Russler, "Eradication Efforts, the State, Displacement and Poverty: Explaining Coca Cultivation in Colombia during Plan Colombia." *Journal of Latin American Studies* 40, no. 3 (2008): 399–421.

instrumental in maintaining coca cultivation numbers in Colombia during the years studied. No such narco-terror groups existed in Peru or Bolivia.30 Thus, Rouse and Arce suggest that additional security assistance is needed to counter the terrorism threat that coincides with drug trafficking in Colombia.

An article titled "A Strategic Framework for Countering Terrorism" by Bruce Hoffman and Jennifer Morrison-Taw similarly argues for the inclusion of a strong governmental security component when addressing the challenges of a terrorist/insurgent population. Hoffman and Taw support the inclusion of a strong government security lead when addressing the insurgent population that funds and supports the illicit crop cultivation. The absence of a consistent government presence or policy toward the narco trafficking organizations and illicit crop farmers will result in an alienated citizenry and a failed government counternarcotic response that allows the narco-traffickers to "exploit the situation to entrench themselves firmly within the population."[31]

Prior to 2006, it was commonly held that policy designed to restrict the supply of drugs would "shift the supply curve up and to the left, increasing the market price and reducing the quantity of drugs sold in the market."[32] Contrary to this belief, the study conducted by Caulkins et al. found that restrictive policies that thin the pool of violent dealers will decrease the likeliness of violence (among dealers), thereby lowering their operating costs. Savings are then passed to the consumer.[33] If correct, this theory would undermine any efforts by the U.S. to pursue security measures as a method of curbing the flow of narcotics into the country.

---

[30] Stella M. Rouse and Moises Arce, "The Drug-Laden Balloon: U.S. Military Assistance and Coca Production in the Central Andes*," *Social Science Quarterly* 87, no. 3 (2006): 555–556.

[31] Bruce Hoffman and Jennifer Morrison-Taw, "A Strategic Framework for Countering Terrorism," in *European Democracies Against Terrorism: Governmental Policies and Intergovernmental Cooperation,* ed. Fernando Reinares (Burlington: Ashgate Publishing Ltd., 2000), 20.

[32] Peter Reuter, and Mark Kleiman, "Risks and Prices: An Economic Analysis of Drug Enforcement," *Crime and Justice: A Review of Research,* vol. 7, (1986): 289–291.

[33] Caulkins, Jonathan P., Peter Reuter, and Lowell J. Taylor. "Can Supply Restrictions Lower Price? Violence, Drug Dealing and Positional Advantage." *B.E.Journal of Economic Analysis and Policy: Contributions to Economic Analysis and Policy* 5, no. 1 (2006): 1.

Based on these quantitative studies, scholars agree that foreign assistance is effective at reducing drug trafficking but disagree on the method of employment. More in-depth process-tracing case studies are needed to address the debate about causal pathways. Thus, this thesis will enhance the understanding of foreign aid's impact on drug trafficking by addressing the debate about what types of aid (security or economic) are most effective and why, using a case study approach.

E.   METHODS AND SOURCES

Colombia was selected for study because it has been the beneficiary of large amounts of U.S. foreign aid for the past decade, and has involved a large range of types of assistance. Colombia has been one of the top annual recipients of U.S. aid since Plan Colombia was initiated in 2000. Between 2000 and 2007, Colombia received approximately $6.2 billion to support Plan Colombia and its initiatives that include: ending the long armed conflict with the Revolutionary Armed Forces of Colombia (FARC) and United Self-Defense Forces of Colombia (AUC); elimination of drug trafficking; and the promotion of economic and social development.[34] Through economic and social development the Clinton administration sought to increase the rule of law, protect human rights, expand economic development, and institute judicial reform in order to eliminate the trafficking of drugs to the U.S.[35]

Data is taken from the Government Accountability Office (GAO), United Nations Office on Drugs and Crime (UNODC) reports, Congressional Research Service reports, USAID, the World Bank, and Pew research reports to examine the impacts of foreign assistance on drug trafficking in Colombia.

---

[34] In addition to being labeled as terrorist organizations, in 2003, the FARC and AUC were designated Significant Foreign Narcotics Traffickers under the Foreign Narcotics Kingpin Designation Act (P.L. 106–120).

[35] U.S. Government Accountability Office, *Plan Colombia: Drug Reduction Goals Were Not Fully Met, but Security Has Improved; U.S. Agencies Need More Detailed Plans for Reducing Assistance* (2008), 28, 47.

F.   THESIS OVERVIEW

This thesis analyzes the results of foreign assistance when applied to Colombia. Plan Colombia and the Andean Counterdrug Initiative are discussed in Chapter II pursuant to counter-narcotic efforts and foreign assistance projects from 2000 to 2011. Chapter III summarizes the findings, correlates results with historical literature, and provides recommendations on how to improve upon current foreign assistance counter-narcotic policy.

II.   COUNTERNARCOTICS ASSISTANCE IN COLOMBIA

A.   BACKGROUND

This chapter will examine the effectiveness of the different components of foreign aid in reducing the amount of cultivated coca in Colombia from 2001 to 2011.   Unlike nearby Peru and Bolivia, which permit the legal cultivation of limited amounts of coca, the Colombian government prohibits coca cultivation entirely. Beginning in the 1970s, the Colombian government devoted significant manpower and resources toward the eradication of coca and poppy plants. Colombia's Direccion Nacional de Estupefacientes (DNE) spearheaded drug control legislation for the country and developed an approach that incorporated "the control of production of coca and poppy; the control of the processing, purification, and transport of the cocaine and heroin; and the seizure and forfeiture of the profits of illicit drug production."[36]   Colombia's drug control policy is neatly aligned with U.S. counternarcotic strategy, save for its exclusion of advancing human rights.

U.S. international narcotics control policy in the early 2000s was focused on reducing "the supply of illicit narcotics flows into the United States," with a secondary aim of reducing "the amount of illicit narcotics cultivated, processed, and consumed worldwide."[37] Prior to Plan Colombia, the U.S. engaged in a large scale coca eradication campaign in Peru and Bolivia. Eradication efforts from 1995 to 2001 successfully eliminated approximately 110,000 hectares of coca, which equated to 70% of the cultivated portions of those countries.[38] During the same period, coca cultivation in Colombia increased by 119,000 hectares (Figure 1). This shift led to major conflicts between well-funded cartels, leftist guerillas, and Colombian law enforcement. In the late

---

[36] Organization of American States, Inter-American Drug Abuse Control Commission, "Environmental and Human Health Assessment of the Aerial Spray Program for Coca and Poppy Control in Colombia," a report prepared for the Inter-American Drug Abuse Control Commission (CICAD) section of the OAS, March 31, 2005, 17.

[37] U.S. Library of Congress, Congressional Research Service, *Drug Control: International Policy and Approaches*, by Raphael Perl, CRS Report IB88093 (Washington, DC: Office of Congressional Information and Publishing, February 2, 2006), 5.

[38] Ibid., 6.

1990s, leftist guerilla groups began heavily taxing the revenue from coca production. This new revenue stream allowed the FARC to expand its control throughout the southeastern portion of the country, eventually controlling more than 40% of Colombia.[39]

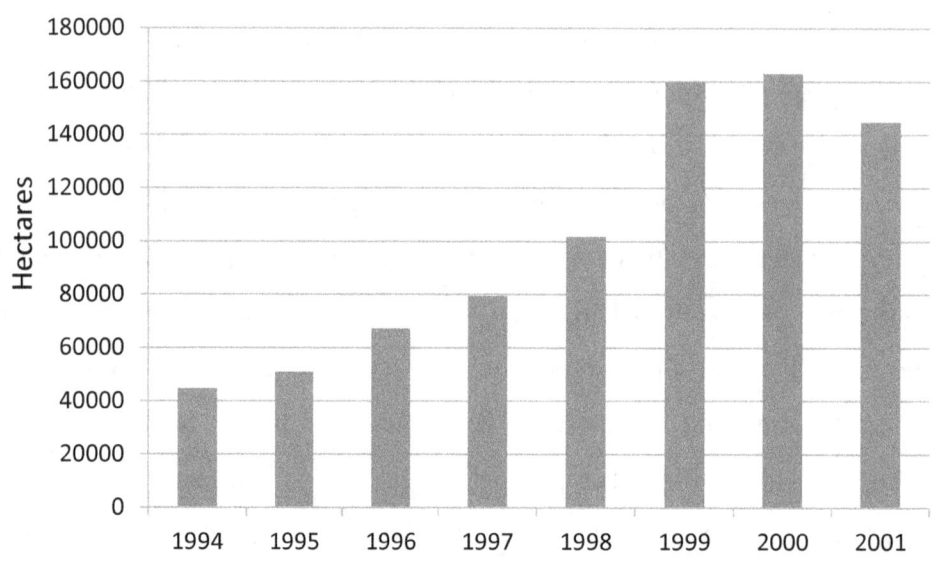

Figure 1.   Coca Cultivated in Colombia from 1994 to 2001

In response to the coca shift into Colombia, U.S. policy makers adopted a new strategy for combating illicit drug trafficking. Working closely with former Colombian President Andrés Pastrana, the U.S. government pledged $2.8 billion for economic assistance and $1.7 billion in Foreign Military Financing (FMF) and Department of Defense assistance for the execution of Plan Colombia.[40]   Security assistance for interdiction and eradication would be complimented by economic assistance for creating alternative cultivation and employment opportunities in Plan Colombia. Plan Colombia adopted a three-pronged approach to curbing cocaine trafficking from Colombia to the United States. The State Department (DoS) assisted the Colombian government with crop eradication activities, the United States Agency for International Development

[39] U.S. Government Accountability Office, *Challenges in Implementing Plan Colombia,* (2000), 1.

[40] U.S. Library of Congress, Congressional Research Service, *Plan Colombia—A Progress Report*, by Connie Veillette, CRS Report RL32774 (Washington, DC: Office of Congressional Information and Publishing, June 22, 2005), i.

(USAID) promoted alternative development paired with governmental reforms, and the Drug Enforcement Agency (DEA) partnered with Colombian counternarcotic officials and U.S. Department of Defense (DoD) specialists to disrupt trafficking organizations and interdict coca shipments.[41]

Although the U.S. did not meet its initial goal of reducing coca cultivation by 50%, Plan Colombia and the Andean Counterdrug Initiative have drastically reduced cultivations numbers from the 1999 to 2001 period, when they were at their all-time high. Figure 2 shows the reduction from 2000 to 2011, with UNODC recording the annual coca cultivation numbers remaining relatively flat after 2004. Of note, the coca cultivation area in 2011 is 60% less than the 163,000 hectares cultivated in 2000. The difficulty for policy makers lies in determining the primary causes of the reduction. Funding for Plan Colombia and the ongoing Andean Counterdrug Initiative was split between eradication, interdiction, and alternative development activities. These factors will be analyzed individually and within the Colombian departments that experienced the most drastic shifts in coca cultivation.

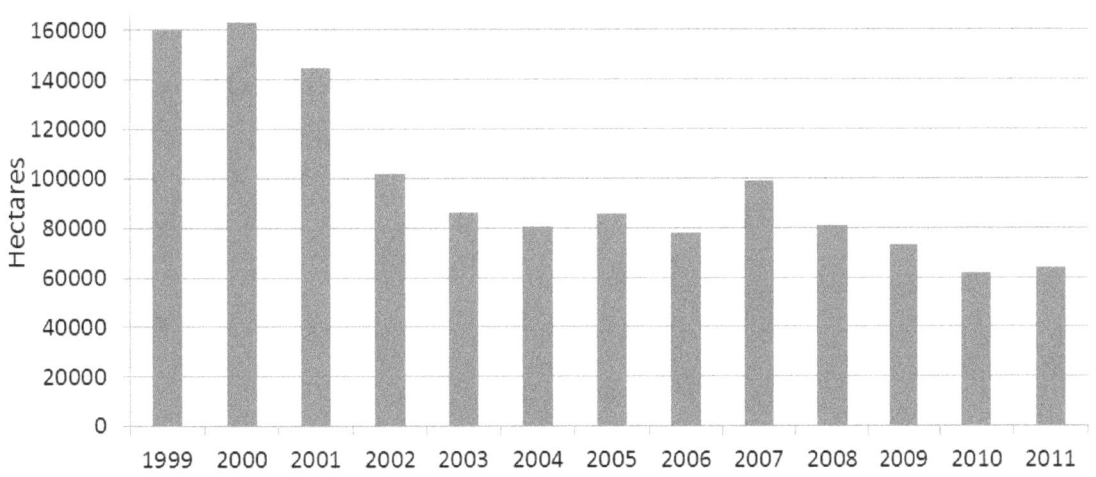

Figure 2.   Coca Cultivated in Colombia since Plan Colombia
and the ACI Were Initiated.

[41] United States Government Accountability Office, *Counter Narcotics Assistance* (2012), 2.

Data for this case study were primarily derived from multi-year United Nations Office of Drug Control (UNODC) Colombia Coca Cultivation Surveys. Analysis of the data entailed the comparison of eradication, alternative development, and security strategies conducted within the different departments of Colombia. The fluctuations in coffee and palm oil prices are also considered as an economic contributor to Plan Colombia's results. Although the oil and mining industry represents approximately 30% of the Colombian export market, it is not considered a significant contributor to employment due to its relatively low employment requirements.[42]

Colombian coca farmers harvest between two and seven times per year. Coastal areas experience fewer yields while higher elevations record the highest number of harvests. The national average yield for a coca plantation is 4.5 times per year or once every 81 days. Annual coca leaf yields (in terms of kilograms per hectare per year) range from 2,600 to 7,100. The national average yield is 4,200 kg/ha/yr.[43] Prior to becoming the cocaine powder that is sold illicitly throughout the world; coca leaves must undergo several chemical processes. Coca leaves are converted into a paste, then a base, and finally into cocaine hydrochloride. The 2012 UNODC Colombia Coca Cultivation Survey indicates that approximately 1.64 kg of cocaine hydrochloride can be derived from one metric ton (mt) of coca leaf. This means that the average hectare of coca plants can produce 2.6kg of cocaine hydrochloride.[44]

---

[42] The combined employment of all Colombian industry, to include oil, textiles, mining, and chemicals, represents only 13% of the labor force; compared to 18% from agriculture alone; *CIA World Factbook*, https://www.cia.gov/library/publications/the-world-factbook/geos/co.html.

[43] United Nations Office of Drug Control, *2012 Colombia Coca Cultivation Survey*, 42-43.

[44] Ibid., 44-45.

	ACI Funding		Interdiction/Security Funding				
	Eradication	Alt Dev	FMF	IMET	NADR	DoD	Total
FY2000	686.40	208.00	—	0.90	—	229.20	1124.50
FY2001	48.00	—	—	1.00	—	190.20	239.20
FY2002	243.50	136.40	—	1.20	25.00	119.10	525.20
FY2003	412.00	168.20	17.10	1.20	3.30	165.00	766.80
FY2004	324.60	159.30	98.50	1.70	0.20	122.00	706.30
FY2005	310.70	152.10	99.20	1.70	5.10	200.00	767.80
FY2006	307.70	157.00	89.10	1.67	5.48	122.00	682.95
FY2007	298.93	166.07	85.50	1.61	3.96	na	556.07
Total	2,631.83	1,147.07	389.40	10.98	43.04	1,147.50	5,368.82

Table 1.   U.S. Funding for Colombia (Millions of USD)[45]

B.   ERADICATION

Eradication is the largest, most costly component of Plan Colombia (Table 1). All eradication efforts are managed and funded by the State Department's Bureau of International Narcotics and Law Enforcement Affairs (INL) and the Narcotics Affairs Section (NAS) of the U.S. Embassy in Colombia.[46] Eradication efforts in Colombia are performed manually and aerially. Manual eradication simply involves uprooting and destroying coca plants by hand. Manual eradication is heavily subsidized by U.S. State Department funding but executed by Mobile Eradication Groups (GME) and the DIRAN.[47] Aerial eradication, often called fumigation, involves low-flying airplanes spraying coca and poppy fields with herbicide. The chemicals destroy the coca leaves, but the root structures remain intact, allowing farmers who prune shortly after a spraying to recommence cultivating activities within six months. Aerial eradication was fully funded by the State Department, and missions were executed by State Department contractors. All aircraft, maintenance, fuel, and herbicide were also provided by the State

---

[45] U.S. Library of Congress, Congressional Research Service, *Andean Counterdrug Initiative and Related Funding Programs: FY2006 Assistance*, by Connie Veillette, CRS Report RL33253 (Washington, DC: Office of Congressional Information and Publishing, January 27, 2006), 6, http://fpc.state.gov/documents/organization/60720.pdf.

[46] U.S. Library of Congress, Congressional Research Service, *Drug Crop Eradication and Alternative Development in the Andes*, by Connie Veillette and Carolina Navarrete-Frias, CRS Report RL33163 (Washington, DC: Office of Congressional Information and Publishing, November. 18, 2005), 3–4; U.S. Government Accountability Office, *Counter Narcotics Assistance*, (2012), 29.

[47] United Nations Office of Drug Control, *2009 Colombia Coca Cultivation Survey*, 73.

Department. The practice of manually uprooting coca plants dates back several decades and was greatly expanded as a component of Plan Colombia. Although more time consuming and requiring considerably more man-power, manual eradication is seen as a superior method of eradication to fumigation because plants are completely destroyed forcing farmers to replant and wait up to eight months for their first yield. Both manual and aerial eradication were utilized prior to 2000, and were greatly expanded with increased U.S. funding. Colombia experienced its all-time high of 163,000 hectares of coca cultivated in 2000. Table 2 illustrates the drastic increase in eradiation activities beginning shortly after Plan Colombia's funding commenced. It is important to note that the area of aerial eradication is often greater than the area of overall coca cultivation (when compared to Figure 1) because many areas are fumigated on numerous occasions during a twelve-month period. Table 2 demonstrates a significant decrease in eradication following 2007's record highs. A 31% decrease in funding for the State Department's eradication efforts in Colombia explains the decrease in aerial eradication volume in 2008. Subsequent years experienced more steady declines in funding that impacted both manual and aerial eradication activities.[48]

---

[48] U.S. Government Accountability Office, *Counter Narcotics Assistance,* (2012), 29.

	2000	2001	2002	2003	2004	2005	2006	2007	2008	2009	2010	2011
Aerial Eradication	58073	94153	130364	132818	136552	138772	172026	153135	133494	104772	101940	130303
Manual Eradication		1745	2752	4011	2589	29746	43536	66377	95732	59071	43690	34172

Table 2.   Total Annual Hectares Eradicated

19

C. INTERDICTION

Interdiction represents the second largest funded component of Plan Colombia (Table 1) and comprised primarily of training and provisions. The State Department, in partnership with DEA and DoD, trained Colombian national police and military forces in tactics for disrupting transnational drug syndicates and illicit drug harvesting terrorist organizations. Interdiction efforts were enhanced by communication and intelligence equipment provided by the State Department. Funding was also earmarked for an increased military presence in previously ungoverned areas of Colombia. Table 3 shows how increased interdiction efforts, as a result of Plan Colombia, have produced drastic increases in cocaine and cocaine derivative seizures. Complementary to Table 3, Table 4 illustrates marked increases in the discovery and subsequent destruction of cocaine production laboratories. Many of the interdiction activities were executed in conjunction with large-scale Colombian military operations such as Plan Patriota and Plan Consolidación. Cocaine, coca base, and coca paste are typically interdicted at labs while coca leaf is seized from both farmers and production facilities. To put this data into perspective, the 2008 seizure of 198,336kg of cocaine HCl is equivalent to the annual average yield of 77,445 hectares of coca.

	2000	2001	2002	2003	2004	2005	2006	2007	2008	2009	2010	2011
Cocaine HCl(kg)	89,856	57,140	95,278	113,142	149,297	173,265	127,326	126,641	198,366	203,166	164,808	155,832
Coca Base (kg)	9,771	16,572	22,615	27,103	37,046	106,491	42,708	33,882	49,663	41,634	46,405	50,401
Coca leaf (kg)	897,911	583,165	638,000	688,691	567,638	682,010	818,544	1,064,503	644,353	826,793	871,249	1,022,532
Coca Paste (kg)	118	53	974	2,368	1,218	2,651	5,451	922	5,001	11,400	3,685	3,892

Table 3.   Cocaine and Cocaine Derivative Seizures

21

	200	200	200	200	200	200	200	200	200	201	201
Labs Destroye	157	144	148	182	193	203	236	320	286	262	240

Table 4.   Cocaine Producing Laboratories Destroyed

D.   ALTERNATIVE DEVELOPMENT

Providing alternate sources of income for former coca farmers was seen as an essential component of Plan Colombia and for the long-term success of illicit crop reduction. Alternative development programs are spearheaded by USAID but executed in cooperation with Colombian government agencies, as well as several non-governmental organizations (NGOs). Colombia is divided into 33 administrative departments (regions). USAID developed economic programs specific to each region based upon climate and geography. The majority of economic programs were not put into place until 2002. Annual funding for Plan Colombia's alternative development programs are listed in Table 1. Data in Table 1 illustrates that security focused eradication and interdiction programs received more than double the funding provided to alternative development initiatives.

Large swaths of Colombia's countryside are devoid of economic infrastructure. Several structural factors limit farmers' ability to grow legitimate crops including "lack of access to land, lack of titles to land, irrigation, roads, credit, technical assistance, and established markets."[49] Cartels and leftist guerilla groups flourish in the ungoverned areas of the country and are willing to support coca farmers who have no access to the structural factors listed above. The three main programs developed to address these shortfalls are Areas for Municipal-Level Alternative Development (ADAM), the Additional Investment for Sustainable Alternative Development (MIDAS), and the Acción Social program. ADAM was implemented in 2005 to reduce illicit crop cultivation through the implementation of sustainable, market-driven, and legitimate

---

[49] USAID, *Assessment of The Implementation of The United States Government's Support for Plan Colombia's Illicit Crop Reduction Components*, Vanda Felbab-Brown et al., Apr 17, 2009, 7.

alternative crop production.[50]   Also initiated in 2005, MIDAS was created to foster entrepreneurialship and legitimate job creation through education and economic reforms. The Acción Social program has many components; the most funded being the Family Forest Warden (Familias Guardabosques) Program. The Family Forest Warden Program (FFWP), created in 2003 to assist families with the abandoning of illicit crops. Participant communities are obligated to eradicate illicit cultivations, not sow or re-sow illicit cultivations, and not carrying out any task related to illegal cultivation whatsoever.[51]   In exchange, the Government of Colombia (GOC) provides bi-monthly payments of 408,000 Colombian Pesos (USD$190) to each family for an 18-month period. The money was designed to cover the loss of revenue from coca and poppy sales until legitimate crops could produce revenue.

Both ADAM and the Family Forest Warden program are essentially contracts with farmers. If the farmer agrees to cease farming illicit crops and demonstrates that all his land is free of coca and poppy, he will be eligible for technical support, marketing assistance, surrounding infrastructure improvements, and seed money to promote the cultivation of licit crops. Additionally, the GOC agreed to subsidize the farmer's revenues until the farmer could reap the benefits of the newly planted legitimate crops.[52] A 2006 State Department report to Congress indicated that "80,000 rural families have benefited from USAID-funded alternative livelihoods projects, generating 53,000 legitimate jobs and more than 100,000 hectares of legitimate crops."[53] A 2010 audit of the alternative development programs in Colombia offered contradictory results. The audit states that only $500.5 million of the $1.015 billion provided by USAID has gone to farmers that desire to switch to a licit crop. One of the difficulties in promoting alternative development lies in how the money is applied to the different communities. A

---

[50] USAID - Office of Inspector General, *Audit of USAID/Colombia's Alternative Development Program*, Mar. 12, 2010, 6.

[51] United Nations Office on Drugs and Crime, *2009 Colombia Coca Cultivation Survey*, 67.

[52] Congressional Research Service, *Drug Crop Eradication and Alternative Development in the Andes*, 7–8.

[53] USAID, *Assessment of The Implementation of The United States Government's Support for Plan Colombia's Illicit Crop Reduction Components*, Vanda Felbab-Brown et al., Apr 17, 2009, 8. http://pdf.usaid.gov/pdf_docs/PDACN233.pdf.

grouping of farms can receive funding only if they first remove all coca plants. If one farmer in the community maintains a small plot of coca then the entire community is cut-off from alternative development funding. The USAID audit summarized the difficulties of applying alternative development by stating, "Communities that benefit from the greatest improvements in security and are least dependent on coca cultivation for economic survival eradicate coca to qualify for GOC and USAID assistance whereas communities that face the greatest insecurity and largest economic obstacles to abandoning coca are left without assistance."[54] Table 5 lists the funding provided to each department from MIDAS and ADAM projects, and each area's corresponding coca cultivation data based upon the USAID audit. The results shown in Table 5 are not promising. Certain departments that received a significant amount of USAID funding experienced large increases in coca cultivation (Cauca) while other departments that received no alternative development funding experienced large decreases in coca cultivation (Arauca).

---

[54] Ibid.

Table 5.　　　Departmental List of Alternative Development Funds Versus Coca Cultivated (From USAID, Assessment of The Implementation of The United States Government's Support for Plan Colombia's Illicit Crop Reduction Components)

Department	No. Coca Hectares 2006	No. Coca Hectares 2008	% Change	Total Value of ADAM and MIDAS Projects in U.S. Dollars
Amazonas	692	836	21	6,042,000
Antioquia	6,157	6,096	-1	24,347,000
Arauca	1,306	447	-66	0
Bolívar	2,382	5,847	145	13,650,000
Boyacá	441	197	-55	1,167,000
Caldas	461	187	-59	791,000
Caquetá	4,967	4,303	-13	31,000
Cauca	2,104	5,422	158	41,752,000
Cesar	0	5		5,735,000
Chocó	816	2,794	242	1,541,000
Córdoba	1,216	1,710	41	10,756,000
Cundinamarca	120	12	-90	15,414,000
Guainía	753	625	-17	0
Guaviare	9,477	6,629	-30	0
La Guajira	166	160	-4	0
Magdalena	271	391	44	1,124,000
Meta	11,063	5,525	-50	0
N. de Santander	488	2,886	491	3,462,000
Nariño	15,606	19,612	26	30,496,000
Putumayo	12,254	9,658	-21	23,991,000
Santander	866	1,791	107	22,988,000
Valle del Cauca	281	2,089	643	1,691,000
Vaupes	460	557	21	0
Vichada	5,523	3,174	-43	0

Alternative development strategies focused largely on the replacement of illicit crops with coffee, oil palm, cut-flowers, cocoa, and sugar. These crops were selected because of their market potential (both domestic and international), as well as the optimal soil and climate conditions found throughout the coca cultivating areas of the country. The following analyzes the impact of oil palm and coffee because they received the most alternative development funding and were correspondingly applied in departments that had a history of extensive coca cultivation.

Coffee is Colombia's leading agricultural export. In the late 1980s, coffee exports represented 51% of Colombia's exports. This resulted in Colombia's acute sensitivity to price fluctuations in the coffee market. Today, coffee remains an important crop with the "livelihoods of an estimated 566,000 families, some 2.3 million Colombians, depending entirely on coffee."[55] Several million people were negatively impacted when international prices of coffee dropped to record lows in 1999–2003. This drop offers a potential explanation for the sudden increase in coca cultivation in 1999. Farmers switched to a more lucrative crop during the coffee price drop. Since 2002, the Colombian government has made strides to prevent such an economic shock from happening again. In 2002 the National Federation of Coffee Growers (Fedecafé) commenced several reforms including,

> commercialization and output-purchase guarantees; stabilization of coffee growers' income; and advancement of coffee institutions by funding R&D, improving the coffee growers' managerial skills, safeguarding Colombian coffee brands in international markets, and developing special coffees.[56]

By 2006, the Colombian economy had diversified into oil, services, and manufacturing exports; leaving coffee at less than 6% of total exports today. Table 6 illustrates annual average coffee export prices and the decrease that occurred in 2001.

---

[55] U.S. Library of Congress, Federal Research Division, *Colombia—A Country Study*, ed. Rex A. Hudson, (Washington, DC: Office of Congressional Information and Publishing, 2010), 6. http://lcweb2.loc.gov/frd/cs/pdf/CS_Colombia.pdf.

[56] Ibid., 153–154.

	1998	1999	2000	2001	2002	2003	2004	2005	2006	2007	2008	2009	2010	2011
US cents/lb	132.40	101.67	85.05	61.91	60.37	64.05	80.09	114.33	113.97	123.25	138.12	141.60	194.37	273.21

Table 6.   Colombian Coffee Prices in U.S. Cents Per Pound

27

Figure 3 graphs the fluctuation in coca cultivation versus coffee bean prices. Fedcafe's reforms, paired with eradication efforts and alternative development programs promoted the legitimate farming of coffee instead of coca. Indeed, many of the alternative development funds went toward promoting coffee as an alternative source of income for impoverished farming families. By 2010, with planning and financial support provided by ADAM, 30,910 hectares were converted from coca to coffee[57].

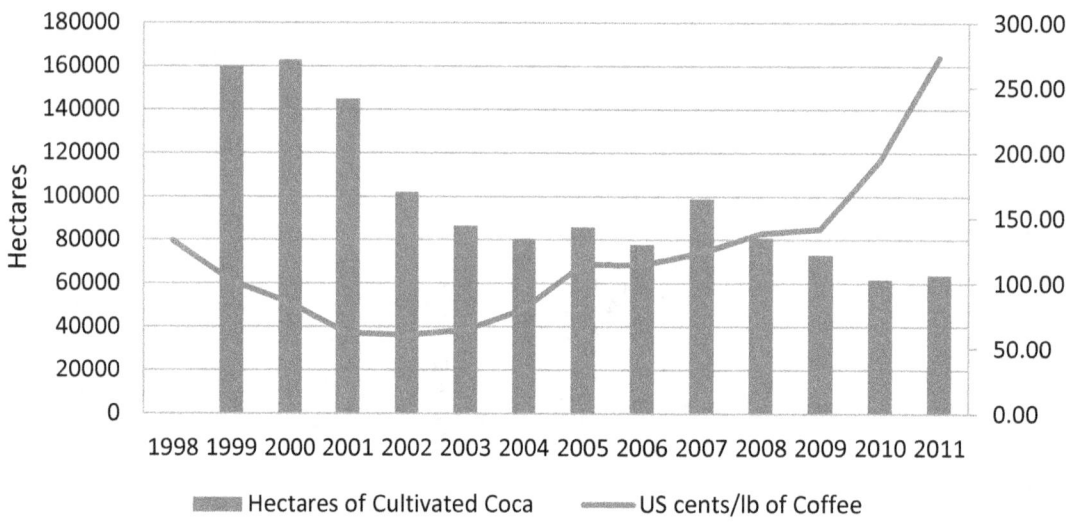

Figure 3.   Coffee Prices Versus the Amount of Cultivated Coca

Oil palm has also been a focus area for alternative development projects. It is primarily grown in the departments of Meta, César, Santander, Nariño, Magdalena, and Norte de Santander. As a result of increased planting and added efficiency measures, Colombia's palm oil yield increased three-fold between 1990 to 2006; placing it among the top five palm oil producing nations in the world. With support from alternative development programs the area of oil palm cultivation has grown to 452435 hectares.[58] Requiring approximately one worker per eight hectares, the palm oil industry employs

[57] USAID—*ADAM Quarterly Performance and Monitoring Report 2010 - 17th Quarter: January – March 2010*, May 5, 2010, 5.

[58] Fedepalma Colombia, "Challenges of Oil Palm Development In Colombia," 3. http://rt10.rspo.org/ckfinder/userfiles/files/P4_3%20Jens%20Mesa-Dishington%20Presentation.pdf

over 130,000 Colombians.[59] The transition from illicit crops to oil palm is a lengthy process, with oil palm trees typically not producing harvestable material until two to four years after initial planting.[60] However, palm oil has proven to be the most successful of alternative development crops due to its diverse uses including food, lotions, medications, and biofuel. It is further supported by the GOC's 2007 implementation of bio-diesel mixing requirements which mandate that all diesels be blended with a 15% mixture of palm oil.[61] In 2011, it was reported that more than 70,000 hectares of coca were replaced with oil palm.[62] Strong domestic demand cushions the palm oil harvesters from significant international market fluctuations in palm oil commodity prices and provides much needed stability for former coca farmers and field hands.

E.   DEPARTMENTAL ANALYSIS

A closer evaluation of specific administrative departments (regions) in Colombia demonstrates which areas experienced the greatest fluctuations in the amount of coca cultivated. Analyzing this data provides insights into the most influential causal factors (eradication, security, or alternative development) involved in the overall coca cultivation reduction from 2000 to 2011. Of the 33 departments in Colombia, 23 are known to have coca fields. Table 7 lists the 23 departments and their corresponding coca cultivation area (in hectares) by year. The highlighted rows, Caquetá, Guaviare, Putumayo, Norte de Santander, and Nariño experienced the greatest fluctuation (in total quantity) over the period studied. In the early stages of the program, these departments accounted for over 80% of the coca cultivated in the country. This table shows an overall decline in coca cultivation from 1999 levels in most of the 23 departments.

---

[59] Ibid., 11; Khoo Khee Ming and D Chandramohan, "Malaysian Palm Oil Industry at Crossroads and Its Future Direction," http://palmoilis.mpob.gov.my/publications/opiejv2n2-10.pdf

[60] Food and Agriculture Organization of the United Nations, "The Oil Palm," http://www.fao.org/docrep/006/T0309E/T0309E01.htm

[61] Nathanial Gronewold, "Biofuels Push Becomes Weapon in Colombia's War on Narco-Traffickers," *New York Times,* May 2, 2011, http://www.nytimes.com/gwire/2011/05/02/02greenwire-biofuels-push-becomes-weapon-in-colombias-war-94778.html?pagewanted=all

[62] Ibid.

Table 7.   Coca Cultivation Changes by Department

	Mar-99	Aug-00	Nov-01	Dec-02	Dec-03	Dec-04	Dec-05	Dec-06	Dec-07	Dec-08	Dec-09	Dec-10
Amazonas			532	784	625	783	897	692	541	836	312	338
Antioquia*	3,644	2,547	3,171	3,030	4,273	5,168	6,414	6,157	9,926	6,096	5,096	5,350
Arauca		978	2,749	2,214	539	1,552	1,883	1,306	2,116	447	430	247
Bolívar	5,897	5,960	4,824	2,735	4,470	3,402	3,670	2,382	5,632	5,847	5,346	3,324
Boyacá		322	245	118	594	359	342	441	79	197	204	105
Caldas					54	358	189	461	56	187	186	46
Caquetá	23,71	26,603	14,516	8,412	7,230	6,500	4,988	4,967	6,318	4,303	3,985	2,578
Cauca	6,291	4,576	3,139	2,120	1,443	1,266	2,705	2,104	4,168	5,422	6,597	5,908
Choco		250	354		453	323	1,025	816	1,080	2,794	1,789	3,158
Cordoba	1,920	117	652	385	838	1,536	3,136	1,216	1,858	1,710	3,113	3,889
Cundinamarca		66	22	57	57	71	56	120	131	12	0	32
Guainia		853	1,318	749	726	721	752	753	623	625	606	446
Guaviare*	28,43	17,619	25,553	27,381	16,163	9,769	8,658	9,477	9,299	6,629	8,660	5,701
La Guajira*		321	385	354	275	556	329	166	87	160	182	134
Magdalena	521	200	480	644	484	706	213	271	278	391	169	121
Meta	11,38	11,123	11,425	9,222	12,814	18,740	17,305	11,063	10,386	5,525	4,469	3,008
Nariño	3,959	9,343	7,494	15,131	17,628	14,154	13,875	15,606	20,259	19,612	17,639	15,951
Norte de Santander	15,03	6,280	9,145	8,041	4,471	3,055	844	488	1,946	2,886	3,037	1,889
Putumayo*	58,29	66,022	47,120	13,725	7,559	4,386	8,963	12,254	14,813	9,658	5,633	4,785
Santander		2,826	415	463	632	1,124	981	866	1,325	1,791	1,066	673
Valle del Cauca		76	184	111	37	45	28	281	453	2,089	997	665
Vaupes	1,014	1,493	1,918	1,485	1,157	1,084	671	460	307	557	395	721
Vichada*		4,935	9,166	4,910	3,818	4,692	7,826	5,523	7,218	3,174	3,228	2,743

30

1. Guaviare

Guaviare is located in the Southeastern portion of Colombia. The terrain is considered *Amazonia* or tropical rainforest. This department had little economic activity until coca cultivation abruptly expanded during the 1980s.[63] By the 1990s, Guaviare was the largest coca cultivating department. Later in the decade, much of the illicit cultivation had moved to nearby Putumayo although Guaviare remained a stronghold of the Revolutionary Armed Forces of Colombia (FARC) members. Population density in the Amazon basin (including Guaviare, Putumayo, and Caquetá) is 0.24 inhabitants per square kilometer.[64] Guaviare represented 27% of the total coca cultivated in 2001.[65] By 2002 it decreased to 19% of the national total. The sizeable reduction in coca cultivation from 2002 to 2004 is largely attributed to the massive increase in aerial eradication. In 2004 President Alvaro Uribe initiated *Plan Patriota,* using a recently quadrupled military force largely funded by U.S. assistance dollars under Plan Colombia. Plan Patriota pushed a large military force into the FARC stronghold in the South and Southeast of Colombia. The military intervention lasted until 2006 when it was replaced by Plan Consolidación. Areas of newly restored security experienced a sustained drop in coca cultivation as a result of the military's continued engagement in the region. Neither MIDAS nor ADAM programs intervened in Guaviare. Figure 4 illustrates how aerial eradication initially decreased cultivation quantities in 2003. The military intervention in 2004 sustained the initial drop in cultivation as aerial eradication efforts decreased. A decline in cartel and leftist guerillas resulted in a smaller customer base for coca farmers. Many coca farmers moved west, further into ungoverned areas near the Ecuador border. Alternative development funding data from FFWP is incomplete but the available data indicates that it was not a large recipient of funds from this program either. Thus, the significant reduction of cultivated coca in Guaviare is largely a result of aerial eradication

---

[63] United Nations Office on Drugs and Crime, *2004 Colombia Coca Cultivation Survey*, 24; Roberto Steiner and Hernán Vallejo, "Agriculture," in *Colombia: A Country Study*, ed. Rex A. Hudson (Washington, DC: Library of Congress Federal Research Division, 2010), 77.

[64] Steiner and Vallejo, *Colombia: A Country Study*, 77, 345.

[65] United Nations Office on Drugs and Crime, *2002 Colombia Coca Cultivation Survey*, 13.

and enhanced security/interdiction. Guaviare coca plantations are smaller and more dispersed due to the military presence, but cocaine production continues to take place in small facilities throughout the department. Today the GOC considers Guaviare "strategically important, not only for coca cultivation, but also as crossing point for both drug trafficking and arms smuggling, as well as for storage of coca base production before export outside the country, due to its vicinity to Venezuela and Brazil."[66]

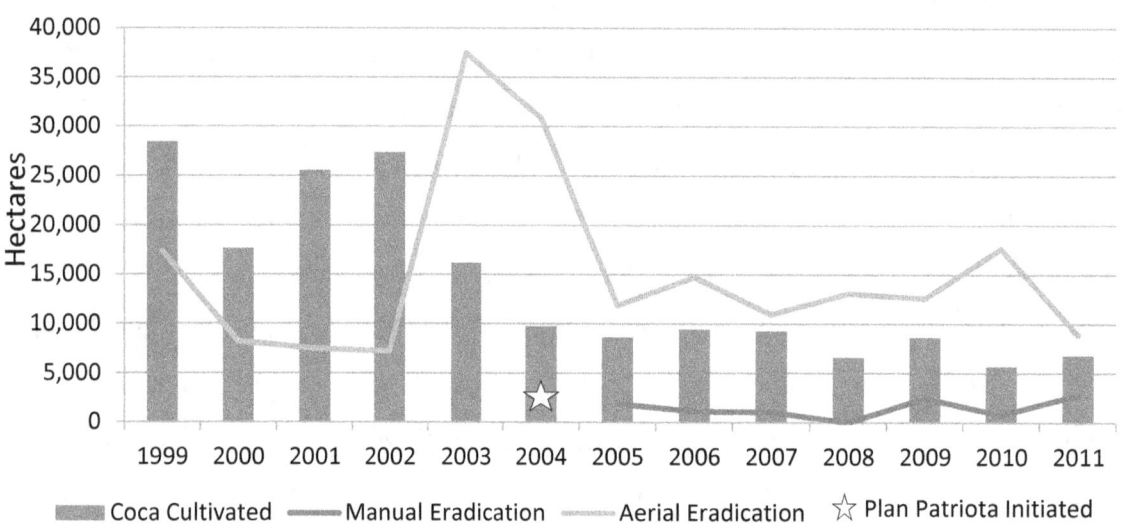

Figure 4. Guaviare Cultivation and Eradication Chart

2. Caquetá

Caquetá borders Guaviare in the South-central portion of Colombia, near the Ecuador border. The western edge is primarily Andean highland, while the central and eastern portions of the department are rain forest. Coca is cultivated almost exclusively in the Andean highlands.[67] There are very few improved surface roads. Several alternative development programs were initiated in Caquetá in 2002.[68] Caquetá received approximately $31,000 from the MIDAS and ADAM programs, the lowest among departments that received aid for the programs. FFWP funds involved several thousand

[66] United Nations Office on Drugs and Crime, *2004 Colombia Coca Cultivation Survey*, 77.

[67] United Nations Office on Drugs and Crime, *2011 Colombia Coca Cultivation Survey*, 12.

[68] United Nations Office on Drugs and Crime, *2013 Colombia Coca Cultivation Survey*, 110.

families; however the program participation greatly decreased by 2010. Due to the minimal funding from MIDAS and ADAM and the subsequent decline in FFWP participation, alternative development programs in Caquetá had no measurable impact. As in Guaviare, the significant reduction of cultivated coca is largely a result of aerial eradication and enhanced security. A large increase in fumigation beginning in 2001, followed by the sustained military presence brought about through Plan Patriota in 2004 have made it very difficult for coca farmers to continue their illicit activities. Additionally, the support provided by cartels and guerillas is greatly diminished because of the enhanced security.

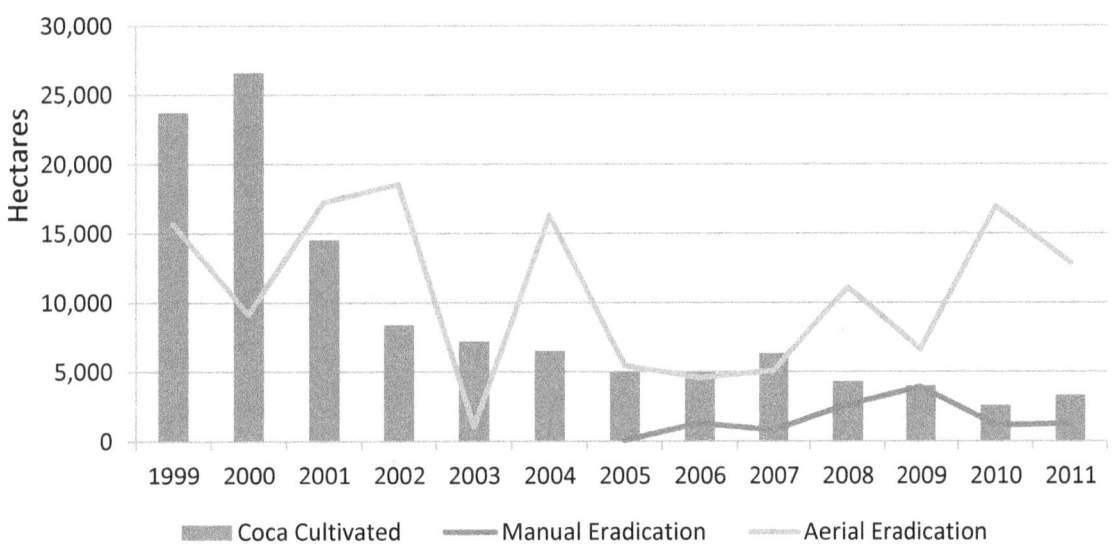

Figure 5.   Caquetá Cultivation and Eradication Chart

3.   Putumayo

Putumayo is located on the southern edge of Colombia, bordering both Ecuador and Peru. The eastern half of Putumayo is Amazonia while the western half is Andean highland. Putumayo's population is 341,513 which represent roughly 0.8% of Colombia's total population.[69] In 1999, Putumayo contained 58,297 hectares of coca, by

---

[69]Gobernacion del Putumayo, www.putumayo.gov.co/nuestro-departamento/informacion-general.html.

far the largest among all 33 departments. In 2000, coca fields in the department expanded to 66,022 hectares, representing 40% of the total coca fields in Colombia. Since 2000, Putumayo has experienced a steady decline in the amount of coca cultivated. In 2011, the UNODC reported that Putumayo's coca cultivation had partially rebounded to 9,951 hectares.[70]

As in the two previous departments Putumayo's coca reduction is largely attributed to an aggressive aerial eradication campaign, followed by an equally aggressive military presence under Plan Patriota and Plan Consolidación. These actions by the GOC have forced guerilla groups and coca farmers into nearby Nariño, which is considerably more remote with very little government presence.[71] Figure 6 illustrates a drastic increase in aerial eradication beginning in 2001, followed by the military presence in 2004, which corresponds with increased cocaine and derivative seizures thereafter. A 2008 assessment of Plan Colombia noted that alternative development strategies have been slow to reach Putumayo. Families that relied on coca for their livelihood either migrated west into Nariño or planted coca seeds in smaller, more remote areas of the department.[72] While Putumayo continues to receive more alternative development funds than most neighboring departments, the implementation of projects and funding Nariño is seen as too slow to continue the coca reduction momentum created by the aggressive aerial eradication campaign. Most alternative development projects take several years before they can begin earning revenue for the targeted population. This overall delay in alternative development explains the fleeting effect of aerial eradication as coca numbers increased 108% in Putumayo from 2010 to 2011.

---

[70] United Nations Office on Drugs and Crime, *2011 Colombia Coca Cultivation Survey*, 10.

[71] United Nations Office on Drugs and Crime, *2002 Colombia Coca Cultivation Survey, 24; Colombia: A Country Study*, 345.

[72] Beatriz Acevedo, Dave Bewley-Taylor, and Coletta Youngers, "Ten Years of Plan Colombia: An Analytic Assessment," *The Beckley Foundation Drug Policy Programme,* September 2008, 10.

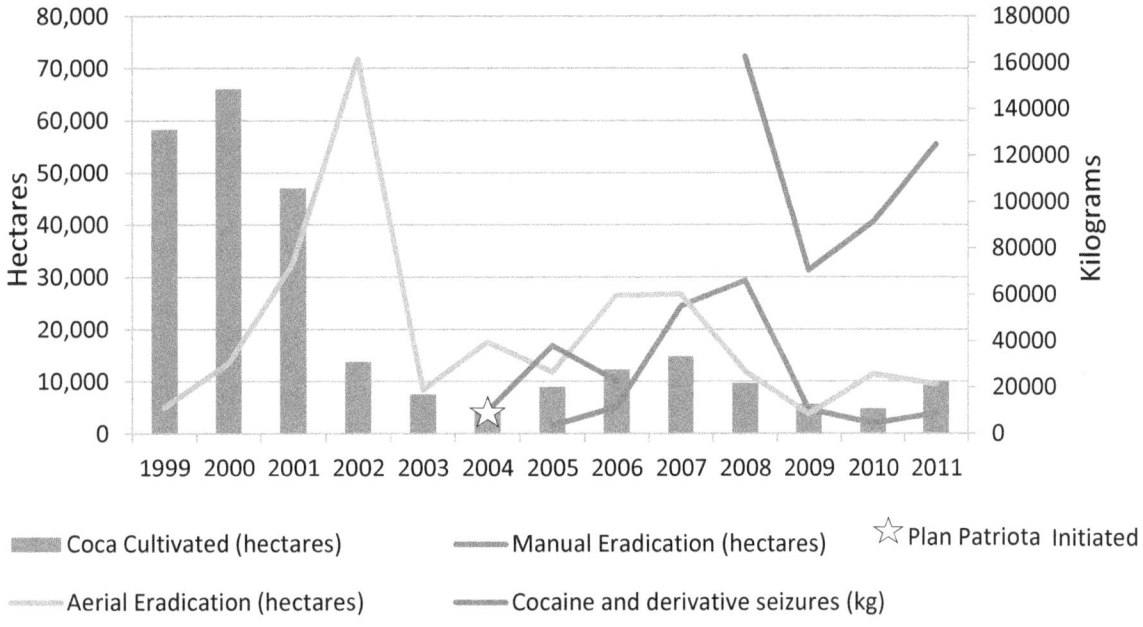

Figure 6.   Putumayo Cultivation, Interdiction, and Eradication Chart

4.   Nariño

Nariño is located in the southwestern edge of Colombia, bordering the Pacific Ocean and Ecuador.   The western edge is considered Pacific lowlands, consisting of jungle and swamps.   The eastern edge is part of the Cordillera Occidental Andean Range with rugged mountainous terrain.   Population density is approximately five inhabitants per square kilometer.[73]   Aside from a few small cities, the department is primarily rural. The Pacific Lowland area offers few roads and little if any state presence.[74]   More than 90% of the coca cultivated in Nariño occurs in the Pacific region.

---

[73] Steiner and Vallejo, *Colombia: A Country Study*, 72.

[74] USAID, *Assessment of Plan Colombia*, 82.

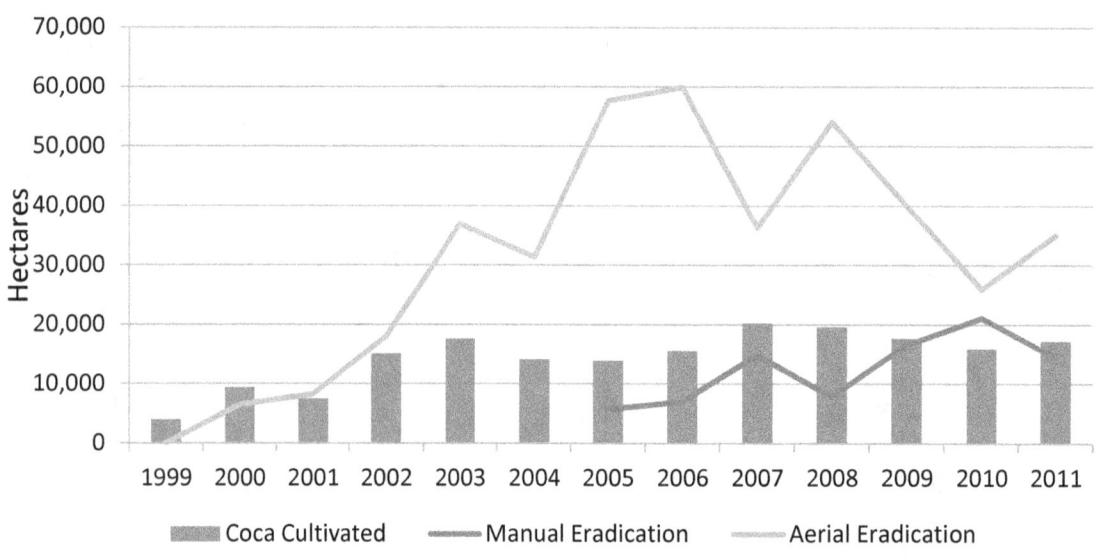

Figure 7.   Nariño Cultivation and Eradication Chart

Figure 7 illustrates that Nariño experienced a 400% increase in coca cultivated from 1999-2010 in spite of significant increases in aerial spraying. The aerial eradication campaign in Nariño was ineffective in large part because of the high level of reseeding in plots that were previously eradicated.[75] Coca cultivating families were driven to replant when they found few alternative development programs to support them. Additionally, Nariño remains a terrorist haven for the FARC and other armed groups that were driven out of Putumayo and Guaviare departments as a result of Plan Patriota.[76] Armed groups actively support coca cultivation in Nariño with their densest concentration of coca cultivation found along the Ecuadorian border. Additionally, aerial eradication efforts in Nariño are stymied by the tenuous relationship between the Ecuadorian government and the Colombian government. Ecuador blames Colombia for accidentally spraying large portions of the border area and destroying legitimate crops. Because of the proximity to the border, Nariño is not able to spray as effectively as it could in other areas.

Several alternative development programs have been initiated in Nariño since 1998. These programs have spent over $52 million, but have failed to produce any long-

---

[75] United Nations Office on Drugs and Crime, *2003 Colombia Coca Cultivation Survey*, 110.

[76] USAID, *Assessment of Plan Colombia*, 84.

36

term reductions in coca cultivation.[77] Alternative development strategies are primarily hindered by a lack of infrastructure and the overall insecurity of the region that has little government presence.[78] Many of the new coca plantations in Nariño were created by former inhabitants of Putumayo, Guaviare, Caquetá, and other departments seeking refuge from persistent aerial eradication and an enhanced security environment that is unfriendly toward coca farmers. A USAID funded analysis of Nariño's counternarcotic strategies found that the marked increase in cultivated coca from Nariño over the past decade is attributed to "an unstable state presence and persisting insecurity, inadequate transport infrastructure, lack of legal livelihood alternatives, including high costs of doing business, and social and geographical isolation."[79] Workers from the three largest alternative development programs are unable to access the southern portions of the department due to instability and violence. Unlike Guaviare, Putumayo, and Caquetá, Plan Patriota and Plan Consolidación did not extend into the Southwestern portion of the country. Legitimate farming activities are unable to succeed with an overall lack of security. Nariño remains the largest coca cultivating department in Colombia today.

5. Norte de Santander

Norte de Santander borders Venezuela on the northeastern edge of Colombia. It is considered Andean highland with a year-round moderate climate, ideal for cultivating numerous types of crops.[80] In 1999, Norte de Santander ranked fourth highest among the coca cultivating departments in Colombia. Up until 2005, the FARC maintained a large presence in the department with little to no government security intervention or investment. Since 2005, the Colombian military has drastically reduced the FARC presence, driving them eastward into Venezuela. Under Plan Consolidación, the military continues to provide security for the department with an ongoing presence spread among

---

[77] USAID, Assessment of Plan Colombia, 96.

[78] Ibid., 93.

[79] Ibid., 87.

[80] *Colombia—A Country Study*, 73–75.

the predominantly rural population centers.[81]   At the start of Plan Colombia Norte de Santander was among the top departments undergoing aerial eradication.   By 2004 both manual and aerial eradication dropped significantly.   This drop in eradication coincides with an increase in alternative development funding as well as an increase in security provided by a persistent military presence.[82]   By 2010, Norte de Santander was the largest recipient department of alternative development funds, receiving over $7 million between 2005 and 2010.[83]   USAID heavily promoted the planting of coffee, oil palm, cocoa, and sugar in the northeast due to its excellent growing conditions.   Figure 8 illustrates a decrease in coca cultivation that coincides with an increase in the commodity price of coffee.   Another significant factor that effected coca cultivation in Norte de Santander was the GOC mandate for 10% bio-diesel mixture in all domestically consumed diesel fuel.   Thus, the significant reduction of cultivated coca in Norte de Santander is largely a result of the combined efforts from eradication, enhanced security, extensive alternative development, and economic conditions that favored more profitable substitutes to coca.

---

[81] Nathanial Gronewold, "Biofuels Push Becomes Weapon in Colombia's War on Narco-Traffickers," *New York Times,* May 2, 2011, http://www.nytimes.com/gwire/2011/05/02/02greenwire-biofuels-push-becomes-weapon-in-colombias-war-94778.html?pagewanted=all.

[82] United Nations Office on Drugs and Crime, *2005 Colombia Coca Cultivation Survey*, 25.

[83] United Nations Office on Drugs and Crime, *2008 Colombia Coca Cultivation* Survey, 64; United Nations Office on Drugs and Crime, *Colombia Monitoreo de Cultivos de Coca 2010*, 69.

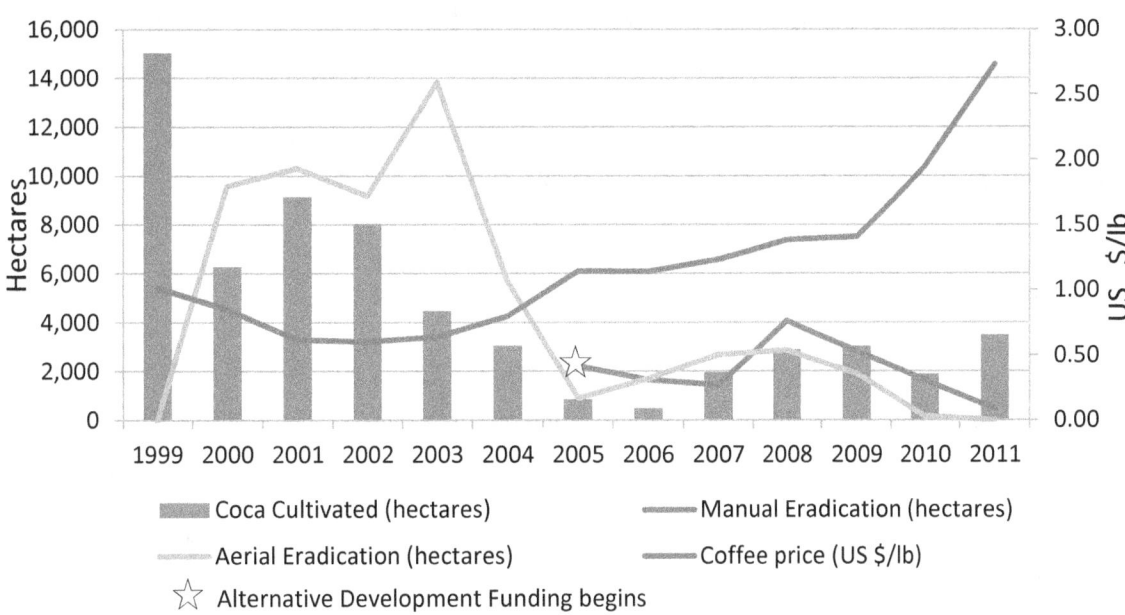

Figure 8.   Norte de Santander Cultivation, Eradication, and Alternative Development Chart

6.   Cauca

Cauca lies along the Pacific coast in the Southwestern corner of Colombia. It borders Nariño in the South, Valle de Cauca in the North, and the Central Cordillera Mountain Range along its eastern edge. It is primarily rural with approximately 1,345,000 inhabitants.[84] In 2007, the GOC began large annual increases in their aerial and manual eradication efforts within Cauca. These activities were not matched with a corresponding decline in illicit crop cultivation. Instead, crop monitoring agencies noted a greater dispersion among coca fields within the department. Numerous small coca plots continue to proliferate in order to minimize the impact of aerial fumigation. Cauca was one of the earliest recipients of U.S. funded alternative development money.[85] From 2005 to 2010 Cauca received USD$41,752,000, which is 27% more than any other department in the nation. Despite all of the alternative development initiatives Cauca experienced minimal fluctuations (both increases and decreases) in the quantity of coca

---

[84] "Inhabitant: Caucano," accessed February 8, 2013, http://www.colombia-sa.com/departamentos/cauca/cauca-in.html.

[85] Congressional Research Service, Andean Counterdrug Initiative and Related Funding Programs: FY2006 Assistance (RL33253: Jan. 27, 2006), Connie Veillette, 6, accessed on Aug. 24, 2012, http://fpc.state.gov/documents/organization/60720.pdf.

cultivated within its borders from 2001 to 2010. However, drastic declines in most of the other departments have slowly elevated Cauca to the second highest coca cultivating department in the nation. Today, Cauca remains the second largest cultivating department, second only to its southern neighbor Nariño. The persistence of coca and opium poppy cultivation in Cauca is mostly attributed to a large FARC and ELN presence.

In 2010 and 2011, the military launched a new round of offensives in Cauca. Military operations were designed to disrupt the longstanding occupation of FARC forces within the department. The military succeeded in killing Alfonso Cano, the leader of the FARC, in November 2011. Although the FARC were dealt a series of defeats, their stronghold remained due to the limited government presence after operations were completed.[86] Unlike Plan Patriota and Plan Consolidación, which sought to establish a long term military/governmental presence, the recent military offensives in South Cauca seek a short term objective and then withdraw back to military headquarters outside the city of Popayán. This strategy only momentarily disrupts the illicit activities of leftist guerillas and cartels that operate in the rural areas of department and does little to influence the agricultural community of Cauca to adopt the licit crop farming practices that were emphasized by alternative development programs.[87]

---

[86] Sarah Maslin Nir and Simon Romero, "Leader of FARC Guerrilla Movement Is Killed in Combat, Colombian Officials Say," *New York Times*, November 5, 2011. http://www.nytimes.com/2011/11/05/world/americas/leader-of-farc-guerrilla-movement-is-killed-in-combat-colombian-officials-say.html?adxnnl=1&adxnnlx=1360276844-n+LCbfPDBSq6Irh2H//7Ew.

[87] Jim Glade, "Drug, Guerrilla Violence Is Crippling Colombia's Southwestern Cauca Department," *New York Times*, April 11, 2011, http://colombiareports.com/colombia-news/news/15526-drug-guerrilla-violence-is-crippling-cauca.html.

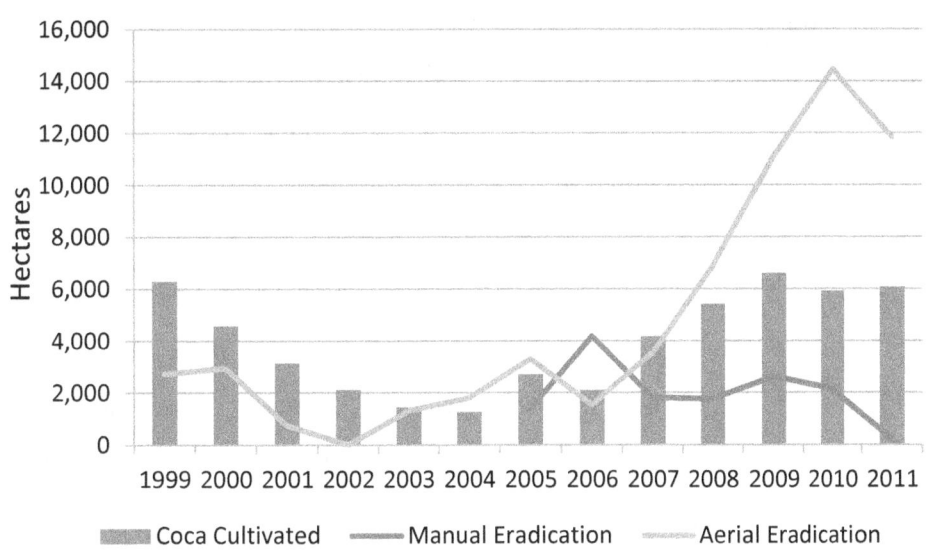

Figure 9.   Cauca Cultivation and Eradication Chart

7.   Departmental Analysis Conclusion

The coca cultivation results from Caquetá, Guaviare, Norte de Santander, Putumayo, Cauca, and Nariño are attributed to different factors; however, security issues demonstrate the largest deciding factor in whether the department experienced an increase or reduction in illicit crop cultivation. After analysis of the economic and security initiatives conducted in Colombia it appears unlikely that alternative development alone is responsible for sustained illicit drug cultivation reductions. Instead, it appears that the programs are mutually dependent on each other for success. The data and interviews with farmers support the use of security/interdiction as the primary reason for the overall reduction in coca cultivation during the period studied. When the military presence increased the coca farmers no longer had an outlet with whom to sell their coca leaves. Departments with little government presence such as Nariño maintain high coca cultivation numbers because the alternative development is not enough to curb the influence of leftist guerillas and cartels.

Developed areas such as Norte de Santander show that alternative development only works when executed in conjunction with significant eradication and interdiction activities. The programs work in tandem to deter coca replanting after eradication efforts

41

are initiated. Cooperation on security initiatives between U.S. and GOC agencies modernized security and justice systems and allowed for the implementation of alternative development programs in many previously hostile rural areas.[88] Impoverished families require a source of income to survive. When eradication/interdiction removes their source of revenue they are encouraged to adopt licit crop farming. Persistent eradication and interdiction raises the risk of being a coca farmer, often leaving a farmer with months of work and nothing to show for it. Alternative development incentives serve as an inducer to legitimize farming activities. However, when eradication is not complemented by alternative development programs, farmers tend to move to an area not impacted by eradication and continue growing coca.[89] Data from the largest coca cultivating departments demonstrates the "balloon effect" whereby one department squeezes out coca cultivation, it expands into another department.[90] This effect continues to push elicit crop planting into the more remote and less-governed areas of Colombia where yields shrink but the threat of eradication and interdiction are greatly diminished. Until such time as the GOC can effectively secure its entire population the coca problem will persist. USAID alternative development projects were not meant to stand alone. They must accompany the disciplinary-styled security measures enacted by the GOC with support from DEA and DoD programs.

---

[88] USAID, *Assessment of The Implementation of The United States Government's Support for Plan Colombia's Illicit Crop Reduction Components*, Vanda Felbab-Brown et al., Apr 17, 2009, iii. http://pdf.usaid.gov/pdf_docs/PDACN233.pdf.

[89] Ibid., 8.

[90] Wayne Bazant, a former UNODC analyst, is credited as the first person to utilize the balloon effect analogy when describing drug production trends in 1987.

III. CONCLUSION

The primary objective of Plan Colombia was to reduce the supply of cocaine going into the U.S. Due to several factors outside of Colombia, cocaine levels in the U.S. remained stable throughout the period analyzed. The government expected to see a price increase as a result of the decreased cocaine availability from counter narcotic initiatives in Colombia. Instead, the 2012 White House report on drug use found that cocaine and derivative prices in the U.S. have experienced an overall decline since their peak in previous decade.[91] During the same period, purity of the cocaine has increased. One factor explaining this price reduction is the increased production of cocaine in Peru and Bolivia.[92] The White House report also indicates a decreased demand for cocaine within the U.S.[93] Thus traditional indicators of supply fluctuations through quantity limitations have not been a reliable benchmark as the Reuter and Kleinman article eluded. This continued availability of cocaine throughout the 2000 to 2011 period provides further credibility to the balloon effect theory.

A.   POLICY IMPLICATIONS

The U.S. greatly benefited from the like-minded policies promoted through Colombia's war on drugs. Similar approaches by the U.S. in Ecuador, Bolivia, and Peru have not come close to achieving the desired results. As indicated earlier, future policies seeking broad economic and security objectives in a foreign nation should only be pursued when the recipient nation's desired end state neatly aligns with that of the U.S. Additionally, the methods of pursuing those objectives must also align. The major disparity between U.S. and GOC counternarcotic policy involved the prioritization of combatting leftist guerilla groups ahead of illicit crop destruction. When developing the objectives for Plan Colombia, the U.S. failed to stress the counter-insurgency component

---

[91] White House, *What America's Users Spend on Illegal Drugs* (Washington, DC: White House, 2012), 59.

[92] United Nations Office on Drugs and Crime, *World Drug Report 2012,* 36.

[93] White House, *Drug Availability Estimates in the United States* (Washington, DC: White House, 2012), 35–36.

of the assistance package. Politicians were led to believe that eradication, interdiction, and alternative development would remedy the widespread illicit crop farming in Colombia. As the U.S. program in Colombia progressed, extensive support to military efforts were required to achieve the desired results. The costly eradication program failed to produce long term reductions in the area of illicit crop cultivation. Similar unilateral attempts at alternative development produced meager results. The foreign assistance funds that were applied to long term military expansion proved to be the most effective starting point for reducing the prevalence of illegal activity (both illicit crops and leftist guerilla groups). These results coincide with the arguments presented by Hoffman and Morrison-Taw.

Since inception, Plan Colombia and the ongoing Andean Counterdrug Initiative have succeeded in reducing the amount of coca cultivated in Colombia. The question for policy makers is: Are the results from Plan Colombia significant enough to warrant continued foreign assistance funding? Policy makers should strongly consider the minimal impact that Plan Colombia had on the availability of cocaine in the U.S. If funding is to continue then policy makers should closely monitor the application of aid funding. As this case study demonstrated, the application of a single component, security, eradication, or alternative development, is rarely enough to turn the population away from illicit crop farming. When the GOC and U.S. partnered to apply both long term security and eradication operations the rural population responded by either adopting legal crops or migrating to a less governed area. The subsequent use of alternative development funds was a critical factor in the process of assisting farmers who desired to adopt legal crops. Financial and infrastructure support allowed the farmers to support their families and provided access to markets for their new crops.

THIS PAGE INTENTIONALLY LEFT BLANK

LIST OF REFERENCES

Acevedo, Beatriz, Dave Bewley-Taylor, and Coletta Youngers. "Ten Years of Plan Colombia: An Analytic Assessment." *The Beckley Foundation Drug Policy Programme,* September 2008, 10. http://www.beckleyfoundation.org/pdf/BriefingPaper_16.pdf.

Ambos, Kai. "Attempts at Drug Control in Colombia, Peru, and Bolivia." *Crime, Law and Social Change* 26, no. 2 (1996): 125–160.

Azam, Jean-Paul and Veronique Thelen. "The Roles of Foreign Aid and Education in the War on Terror." *Public Choice* 135, no. 3-4 (2008): 375–397.

Becker, Gary S. "Crime and Punishment: An Economic Approach." *Journal of Political Economy* 76, no. 2 (March 1968): 169–217.

Behrman, Greg. *The Most Noble Adventure: The Marshall Plan and the Time When America Helped Save Europe.* New York: Free Press, 2007.

Byman, Daniel. *The Five Front War.* Hoboken: John Wiley & Sons, 2008.

Caulkins, Jonathan P., Peter Reuter, and Lowell J. Taylor. "Can Supply Restrictions Lower Price? Violence, Drug Dealing and Positional Advantage."*Contributions to Economic Analysis & Policy* 5, no. 1 (2006): 1–18.

Cohen, Paul,T. "The Post-Opium Scenario and Rubber in Northern Laos: Alternative Western and Chinese Models of Development." *International Journal of Drug Policy* 20, no. 5 (2009): 424–430.

Colombia-SA."Inhabitant: Caucano," accessed February 8, 2013. http://www.colombia-sa.com/departamentos/cauca/cauca-in.html.

Cromwell, William C. "The Marshall Non-Plan, Congress and the Soviet Union." *Western Political Quarterly* 32, no. 4 (1979): 422–443.

Cronin, Patrick M. "Foreign Aid," in *Attacking Terrorism: Elements of a Grand Strategy,* edited by Audrey Kurth Cronin and James M. Ludes, 248–249. Washington, D.C.: Georgetown University Press, 2004.

Dion, Michelle L. and Catherine Russler, "Eradication Efforts, the State, Displacement and Poverty: Explaining Coca Cultivation in Colombia during Plan Colombia." *Journal of Latin American Studies* 40, no. 3 (2008): 399–421.

Drakos, Konstantinos and Andreas Gofas. "In Search of the Average Transnational Terrorist Attack Venue." *Defence and Peace Economics* 17, no. 2 (2006): 73–93.

Farrell, Graham. "A Global Empirical Review of Drug Crop Eradication and United Nations Crop Substitution and Alternative Development Strategies." *Journal of Drug Issues* 28, no. 2 (1998): 395–395.

Fedepalma Colombia. "Challenges of Oil Palm Development in Colombia." http://rt10.rspo.org/ckfinder/userfiles/files/P4_3%20Jens%20Mesa-Dishington%20Presentation.pdf

Food and Agriculture Organization of the United Nations. "The Oil Palm," http://www.fao.org/docrep/006/T0309E/T0309E01.htm

Gardner, Royal C. International Assistance, Sustainable Development, and the War on Terrorism. Washington, D.C.: Environmental Law Institute, 2002.

Glade, Jim. "Drug, Guerrilla Violence is Crippling Colombia's Southwestern Cauca Department," *New York Times*, April 11, 2011.

Gronewold, Nathanial. "Biofuels Push Becomes Weapon in Colombia's War on Narco-Traffickers." *New York Times,* May 2, 2011.

Hastings, Tom H. *Nonviolent Response to Terrorism.* Jefferson: McFarland & Company, 2004.

Hoffman, Bruce and Jennifer Morrison-Taw. "A Strategic Framework for Countering Terrorism" in *European Democracies Against Terrorism: Governmental Policies and Intergovernmental Cooperation,* edited by . Fernando Reinares (Burlington: Ashgate Publishing Ltd., 2000), 3–29.

International Trade Centre,"Trade Map." accessed October 8, 2012. http://www.trademap.org/tradestat/Country_SelProduct_TS.aspx

Jeffcoat, A. E. "Dollars for Europe." *Wall Street Journal,* April 11, 1951.

Lacquement, Richard A. Jr. "Integrating Civilian and Military Activities." *Parameters* 41, no. 4 (2011): 128–139.

Levinson, Jerome and Juan de Onis. *The Alliance That Lost Its Way.* Chicago: Quadrangle Books, 1970.

Lum, Cynthia, Leslie W. Kennedy, and Alison Sherley. "Are Counter-Terrorism Strategies Effective? The Results of the Campbell Systematic Review on Counter-Terrorism Evaluation Research." *Journal of Experimental Criminology* 2, no. 4 (2006): 508–512.

Maslin Nir, Sarah and Simon Romero. "Leader of FARC Guerrilla Movement Is Killed in Combat, Colombian Officials Say." *New York Times*, November 5, 2011.

Khoo Khee, M., and D. Chandramohan. "Malaysian Palm Oil Industry at Crossroads and Its Future Directions." *Palm Oil Industry Economic Journal* 2, no. 2 (2002): 10-15. http://palmoilis.mpob.gov.my/publications/opiejv2n2-10.pdf

Organization of American States - Inter-American Drug Abuse Control Commission. "Environmental and Human Health Assessment of the Aerial Spray Program for Coca and Poppy Control in Colombia." a report prepared for the Inter-American Drug Abuse Control Commission (CICAD) section of the OAS, March 31, 2005. http://www.cicad.oas.org/mem/reports/5/Full_Eval/Colombia%20-%205th%20Rd%20-%20ENG.pdf.

Rabe, Stephen C. The Most Dangerous Area in the World—John F. Kennedy Confronts Communist Revolution in Latin America.Chapel Hill: The University of North Carolina Press, 1999.

Reuter, Peter and Mark Kleiman. "Risks and Prices: An Economic Analysis of Drug Enforcement." Weinstein, Joshua I. "The Market in Plato's *Republic.*" *Crime and Justice: A Review of Research,* vol. 7 (1986): 289–340.

Rouse, Stella M. and Moises Arce. "The Drug-Laden Balloon: U.S. Military Assistance and Coca Production in the Central Andes*."*Social Science Quarterly* 87, no. 3 (2006): 540–557. http://search.proquest.com/docview/204359178?accountid=12702.

Roberto Steiner and Hernán Vallejo, "Agriculture," in *Colombia: A Country Study* (Washington, D.C.: Library of Congress Federal Research Division, 2010) http://lcweb2.loc.gov/frd/cs/pdf/CS_Colombia.pdf.

Sachs, Jeffrey D. "The Strategic Significance of Global Inequality." *Washington Quarterly* 24, no. 3 (2001): 187–198.

Savun, Burcu and Hays, Jude C., Foreign Aid as a Counterterrorism Tool: Aid Delivery Channels, State Capacity, and NGOs (2011). APSA 2011 Annual Meeting Paper. http://ssrn.com/abstract=1900690

Smith, Peter H. *Talons of the Eagle: Dynamics of U.S.-Latin American Relations.* New York: Oxford University Press, 1996.

United Nations Office on Drugs and Crime. *Coca Cultivation In The Andean Region 2007.* June 2008. http://www.unodc.org/unodc/en/crop-monitoring/index.html

———. *Colombia Coca Cultivation Survey 2003.* June 2004. http://www.unodc.org/unodc/en/crop-monitoring/index.html

———. *Colombia Coca Cultivation Survey 2004.* http://www.unodc.org/unodc/en/crop-monitoring/index.html

————. *Colombia Coca Cultivation Survey 2005*. http://www.unodc.org/unodc/en/crop-monitoring/index.html

————. *Colombia Coca Cultivation Survey 2006*. http://www.unodc.org/unodc/en/crop-monitoring/index.html

————. *Colombia Coca Cultivation Survey 2008*. http://www.unodc.org/unodc/en/crop-monitoring/index.html

————. *Colombia Coca Cultivation Survey 2009*. http://www.unodc.org/unodc/en/crop-monitoring/index.html

————. *Colombia Coca Cultivation Survey 2010*. http://www.unodc.org/unodc/en/crop-monitoring/index.html

————. *Colombia Coca Cultivation Survey 2011*. http://www.unodc.org/unodc/en/crop-monitoring/index.html

————. *World Drug Report 2012*. http://www.unodc.org/documents/data-and-analysis/WDR2012/WDR_2012_web_small.pdf.

USAID. *ADAM Quarterly Performance and Monitoring Report 2010 - 17th Quarter: January – March 2010*. Burlington, VT: ARD Incorporated, 2010. http://pdf.usaid.gov/pdf_docs/PDACQ994.pdf.

————. *Assessment of the Implementation of the United States Government's Support For Plan Colombia's Illicit Crop Reduction Components*. by Vanda Felbab-Brown, Joel M. Jutkowitz, Sergio, Rivas, Ricardo Rocha, James T. Smith, Manuel Supervielle, and Cynthia Watson. Washington, DC: Management Systems International, 2009. http://pdf.usaid.gov/pdf_docs/PDACN233.pdf.

U.S. Government Accountability Office. *Counter Narcotics Assistance,* by Charles M. Johnson. GAO-12-824. 2012. http://www.gao.gov/assets/600/592241.pdf.

————. *Drug Control: Challenges in Implementing Plan Colombia,* by Jess T. Ford. GAO-01-76T. 2000. http://www.gao.gov/assets/110/108704.pdf.

————. *Plan Colombia: Drug Reduction Goals Were Not Fully Met, but Security Has Improved; U.S. Agencies Need More Detailed Plans for Reducing Assistance*, by Jess T. Ford. GAO-09-71. 2008. http://www.gao.gov/assets/290/282511.pdf.

USAID Office of Inspector General. *Audit of USAID/Colombia's Alternative Development Program*. by Catherine Trujillo. Report no. 1-514-10-004-P. San Salvador, El Salvador: n.p., 2010. http://oig.usaid.gov/sites/default/files/audit-reports/1-514-10-004-p.pdf.

U.S. Library of Congress. Congressional Research Service. *Andean Counterdrug Initiative and Related Funding Programs: FY2006 Assistance* by Connie Veillette. CRS Report RL33253. Washington, DC: Office of Congressional Information and Publishing, January 27, 2006.

———. Congressional Research Service. *Drug Control: International Policy and Approaches* by Raphael Perl. CRS Report IB88093. Washington, DC: Office of Congressional Information and Publishing, February 2, 2006.

———. Congressional Research Service. *Drug Crop Eradication and Alternative Development in the Andes,* by Connie Veillette and Carolina Navarrete-Frias. CRS Report RL33163. Washington, DC: Office of Congressional Information and Publishing, November 18, 2005.

———. Congressional Research Service. *Plan Colombia – A Progress Report*, by Connie Veillette. RL32774. Washington, DC: Office of Congressional Information and Publishing, June. 22, 2005.

U.S. Library of Congress Federal Research Division. *Colombia-A Country Study*. Edited by Rex A. Hudson. Area Handbook Series. Washington, DC: U.S. Government Printing Office, 2010. http://lcweb2.loc.gov/frd/cs/pdf/CS_Colombia.pdf.

White House. *Drug Availability Estimates in the United States.* Washington, DC: White House, 2012. *http://www.whitehouse.gov/sites/default/files/page/files/daeus_report_final_1.pdf.*

———.*National Security Strategy.* Washington, DC: White House, 2010.http://www.whitehouse.gov/sites/default/files/rss_viewer/national_security_strategy.pdf.

———. *National Security Strategy of the United States*. Washington, DC: White House, 1993. http://nssarchive.us/NSSR/1993.pdf

———. *A National Security Strategy for a New Century.* Washington, DC: White House, 1997. http://nssarchive.us/NSSR/1997.pdf

———. *The National Security Strategy of the United States of America.* Washington, DC: White House, 2002. http://nssarchive.us/NSSR/2002.pdf

———. *The National Security Strategy of the United States of America.* Washington, DC: White House, 2006. http://nssarchive.us/NSSR/2006.pdf

White House. *National Security Strategy.* Washington, DC: White House, 2010. http://nssarchive.us/NSSR/2010.pdf

White House. *National Drug Control Strategy*. Washington, DC: White House, 2012. http://www.whitehouse.gov/sites/default/files/ondcp/2012_ndcs.pdf

White House. *What America's Users Spend on Illegal Drugs.* Washington, DC: White
    House, 2012.
    http://www.whitehouse.gov/sites/default/files/page/files/wausid_report_final_1.pd
    f.

Wright, Thomas C. *Latin America in the era of the Cuban Revolution.* Westport: Praeger
    Publishers, 2001.

Zentner, Joseph L. "The 1972 Turkish Opium Ban: Needle in the Haystack Diplomacy?
    [Efforts to Curtail Production; Effects on the Illicit Drug Market; Effects on the
    Turkish Economy; Efforts to Aid Poppy Farmers Affected by the Ban]." *World
    Affairs* 136, (1973): 36-47.